THE CARRYING

THE CARRYING

POEMS

ADA LIMÓN

MILKWEED EDITIONS

Published 2018 by Milkweed Editions
Printed in Canada
Cover design by Mary Austin Speaker
Cover art by Stacia Brady
Author photo by Lucas Marquardt
19 20 21 22 5 4 3
First Edition

Milkweed Editions, an independent nonprofit publisher, gratefully acknowledges sustaining support from the Jerome Foundation; the Lindquist & Vennum Foundation; the McKnight Foundation; the National Endowment for the Arts; the Target Foundation; and other generous contributions from foundations, corporations, and individuals. Also, this activity is made possible by the voters of Minnesota through a Minnesota State Arts Board Operating Support grant, thanks to a legislative appropriation from the arts and cultural heritage fund, and a grant from Wells Fargo. For a full listing of Milkweed Editions supporters, please visit milkweed.org.

Library of Congress Cataloging-in-Publication Data

Names: Limón, Ada, author.
Title: The carrying : poems / Ada Limón.
Description: First edition. | Minneapolis, Minnesota : Milkweed Editions, 2018. | Includes bibliographical references.
Identifiers: LCCN 2017061361 (print) | LCCN 2018002212 (ebook) | ISBN 9781571319944 (ebook) | ISBN 9781571315120 (hardcover : acid-free paper)
Classification: LCC PS3612.I496 (ebook) | LCC PS3612.I496 A6 2018 (print) | DDC 811/.6--dc23
LC record available at https://lccn.loc.gov/2017061361

Milkweed Editions is committed to ecological stewardship. We strive to align our book production practices with this principle, and to reduce the impact of our operations in the environment. We are a member of the Green Press Initiative, a nonprofit coalition of publishers, manufacturers, and authors working to protect the world's endangered forests and conserve natural resources. *The Carrying* was printed on acid-free 100% postconsumer-waste paper by Friesens Corporation.

For Lucas & Lily Bean

CONTENTS

1.

A Name . 3

Ancestors . 4

How Most of the Dreams Go . 5

The Leash . 6

Almost Forty . 8

Trying . 9

On a Pink Moon . 10

The Raincoat . 11

The Vulture & the Body . 12

American Pharoah . 14

Dandelion Insomnia . 16

Dream of the Raven . 17.

The Visitor . 18

Late Summer after a Panic Attack . 19

Bust . 20

Dead Stars . 22

Dream of Destruction . 24

Prey . 25

2.

The Burying Beetle . 29

How We Are Made . 31

The Light the Living See . 32

The Dead Boy . 34

What I Want to Remember . 36

Overpass . 38

The Millionth Dream of Your Return . 39

Bald Eagles in a Field . 40

I'm Sure about Magic . 41

Wonder Woman . 42

The Real Reason . 43

The Year of the Goldfinches . 45

Notes on the Below . 46

Sundown & All the Damage Done . 48

On a Lamppost Long Ago . 49

Of Roots & Roamers . 51

Killing Methods . 53

Full Gallop . 54

Dream of the Men . 55

A New National Anthem . 56

Cargo . 58

The Contract Says: We'd Like the Conversation to Be Bilingual . 60

It's Harder . 62

3.

Against Belonging . 65

Instructions on Not Giving Up . 66

Would You Rather . 67

Maybe I'll Be Another Kind of Mother . 69

Carrying . 70

What I Didn't Know Before . 71

Mastering . 72

The Last Thing . 74

Love Poem with Apologies for My Appearance . 75

Sway . 76

Sacred Objects . 78

Sometimes I Think My Body Leaves a Shape in the Air . 79

Cannibal Woman . 81

Wife . 83
From the Ash inside the Bone . 84
Time Is On Fire . 86
After the Fire . 87
Losing . 88
The Last Drop . 89
After His Ex Died . 90
Sparrow, What Did You Say? . 91

Notes & Acknowledgments . 93

She had some horses she loved.
She had some horses she hated.

These were the same horses.

JOY HARJO

THE CARRYING

I

A NAME

When Eve walked among
the animals and named them—
nightingale, red-shouldered hawk,
fiddler crab, fallow deer—
I wonder if she ever wanted
them to speak back, looked into
their wide wonderful eyes and
whispered, *Name me, name me.*

ANCESTORS

I've come here from the rocks, the bone-like chert,
        obsidian, lava rock. I've come here from the trees—

chestnut, bay laurel, toyon, acacia, redwood, cedar,

one thousand oaks
        that bend with moss and old-man's beard.
I was born on a green couch on Carriger Road between
        the vineyards and the horse pasture.

I don't remember what I first saw, the brick of light
        that unhinged me from the beginning. I don't remember

my brother's face, my mother, my father.

        Later, I remember leaves, through car windows,
through bedroom windows, through the classroom window,

the way they shaded and patterned the ground, all that
        power from roots. Imagine you must survive

without running? I've come from the lacing patterns of leaves,

        I do not know where else I belong.

HOW MOST OF THE DREAMS GO

First, it's a fawn dog, and then
it's a baby. I'm helping him

to swim in a thermal pool,
the water is black as coffee,

the cement edges are steep
so to sink would be easy

and final. I ask the dog
(that is also the child),

Is it okay that I want
you to be my best friend?

And the child nods.
(And the dog nods.)

Sometimes, he drowns.
Sometimes, we drown together.

THE LEASH

After the birthing of bombs of forks and fear,
the frantic automatic weapons unleashed,
the spray of bullets into a crowd holding hands,
that brute sky opening in a slate-metal maw
that swallows only the unsayable in each of us, what's
left? Even the hidden nowhere river is poisoned
orange and acidic by a coal mine. How can
you not fear humanity, want to lick the creek
bottom dry, to suck the deadly water up into
your own lungs, like venom? Reader, I want to
say: *Don't die.* Even when silvery fish after fish
comes back belly up, and the country plummets
into a crepitating crater of hatred, isn't there still
something singing? The truth is: I don't know.
But sometimes I swear I hear it, the wound closing
like a rusted-over garage door, and I can still move
my living limbs into the world without too much
pain, can still marvel at how the dog runs straight
toward the pickup trucks breaknecking down
the road, because she thinks she loves them,
because she's sure, without a doubt, that the loud
roaring things will love her back, her soft small self
alive with desire to share her goddamn enthusiasm,
until I yank the leash back to save her because
I want her to survive forever. *Don't die*, I say,
and we decide to walk for a bit longer, starlings
high and fevered above us, winter coming to lay
her cold corpse down upon this little plot of earth.
Perhaps we are always hurtling our bodies toward
the thing that will obliterate us, begging for love

from the speeding passage of time, and so maybe,
like the dog obedient at my heels, we can walk together
peacefully, at least until the next truck comes.

ALMOST FORTY

The birds were being so bizarre today,
we stood static and listened to them insane

in their winter shock of sweet gum and ash.
We swallow what we won't say: *Maybe*

it's a warning. Maybe they're screaming
for us to take cover. Inside, your father

seems angry, and the soup's grown cold
on the stove. I've never been someone

to wish for too much, but now I say,
I want to live a long time. You look up

from your work and nod. *Yes, but*
in good health. We turn up the stove

again and eat what we've made together,
each bite an ordinary weapon we wield

against the shrinking of mouths.

TRYING

I'd forgotten how much
I like to grow things, I shout
to him as he passes me to paint
the basement. I'm trellising
the tomatoes in what's called
a Florida weave. Later, we try
to knock me up again. We do it
in the guest room because that's
the extent of our adventurism
in a week of violence in Florida
and France. Afterward,
the sun still strong though lowering
inevitably to the horizon, I check
on the plants in the back, my
fingers smelling of sex and tomato
vines. Even now, I don't know much
about happiness. I still worry
and want an endless stream of more,
but some days I can see the point
in growing something, even if
it's just to say I cared enough.

ON A PINK MOON

I take out my anger
And lay its shadow

On the stone I rolled
Over what broke me.

I plant three seeds
As a spell. One

For what will grow
Like air around us,

One for what will
Nourish and feed,

One for what will
Cling and remind me—

We are the weeds.

THE RAINCOAT

When the doctor suggested surgery
and a brace for all my youngest years,
my parents scrambled to take me
to massage therapy, deep tissue work,
osteopathy, and soon my crooked spine
unspooled a bit, I could breathe again,
and move more in a body unclouded
by pain. My mom would tell me to sing
songs to her the whole forty-five-minute
drive to Middle Two Rock Road and forty-
five minutes back from physical therapy.
She'd say that even my voice sounded unfettered
by my spine afterward. So I sang and sang,
because I thought she liked it. I never
asked her what she gave up to drive me,
or how her day was before this chore. Today,
at her age, I was driving myself home from yet
another spine appointment, singing along
to some maudlin but solid song on the radio,
and I saw a mom take her raincoat off
and give it to her young daughter when
a storm took over the afternoon. My god,
I thought, my whole life I've been under her
raincoat thinking it was somehow a marvel
that I never got wet.

THE VULTURE & THE BODY

On my way to the fertility clinic,
                I pass five dead animals.

First a raccoon with all four paws to the sky
            like he's going to catch whatever bullshit load
falls on him next.

Then, a grown coyote, his golden furred body soft against the white
            cement lip of the traffic barrier. Trickster no longer,
an eye closed to what's coming.

Close to the water tower that says "Florence, Y'all," which means
I'm near Cincinnati, but still in the bluegrass state,
                and close to my exit, I see

three dead deer, all staggered but together, and I realize as I speed
past in my death machine that they are a family. I say something

to myself that's between a prayer and a curse—how dare we live
                on this earth.

I want to tell my doctor about how we all hold a duality
            in our minds: futures entirely different, footloose or forged.

I want to tell him how lately, it's enough to be reminded that my
body is not just my body, but that I'm made of old stars and so's he,
            and that last Tuesday,

I sat alone in the car by the post office and just *was*
        for a whole hour, no one knowing how to find me, until
I got out, the sound of the car door shutting like a gun,

and mailed letters, all of them saying, *Thank you.*

But in the clinic, the sonogram wand showing my follicles, he asks
if I have any questions, and says, *Things are getting exciting.*

I want to say, *But what about all the dead animals?*

But he goes quicksilver, and I'm left to pull my panties up like a big girl.

Some days there is a violent sister inside of me, and a red ladder
        that wants to go elsewhere.

I drive home on the other side of the road, going south now.
The white coat has said I'm ready, and I watch as a vulture
        crosses over me, heading toward

the carcasses I haven't properly mourned or even forgiven.
        What if, instead of carrying

    a child, I am supposed to carry grief?

The great black scavenger flies parallel now, each of us speeding,
intently and driven, toward what we've been taught to do with death.

AMERICAN PHAROAH

Despite the morning's gray static of rain,
we drive to Churchill Downs at 6 a.m.,
eyes still swollen shut with sleep. I say,
Remember when I used to think everything
was getting better and better? Now I think
it's just getting worse and worse. I know it's not
what I'm supposed to say as we machine our
way through the silent seventy minutes on 64
over potholes still oozing from the winter's
wreckage. I'm tired. I've had vertigo for five
months and on my first day home, he's shaken
me awake to see this horse not even race, but
work. He gives me his jacket as we face
the deluge from car to the Twin Spire turnstiles,
and once deep in the fern-green grandstands I see
the crowd. A few hundred maybe, black umbrellas,
cameras, and notepads, wet-winged eager early birds
come to see this Kentucky-bred bay colt with his
chewed-off tail train to end the almost forty-year
American Triple Crown drought. A man next to us,
some horse racing bigwig, hisses a list of reasons
why this horse—his speed-heavy pedigree, muscle
and bone recovery, etcetera etcetera could never
win the grueling mile-and-a-half Belmont Stakes.
Then the horse comes out, first just casually trotting
with his lead horse, and all at once, a brief break
in the storm, and he's racing against no one
but himself and the official clockers, monstrously
fast and head down so we can see that faded star
flash on his forehead like this is real gladness.

As the horse eases up and all of us close our mouths
to swallow, the big-talking guy next to us folds his arms,
says what I want to say too: *I take it all back.*

DANDELION INSOMNIA

The big-ass bees are back, tipsy, sun drunk
and heavy with thick knitted leg warmers
of pollen. I was up all night again so today's
yellow hours seem strange and hallucinogenic.
The neighborhood is lousy with mowers, crazy
dogs, and people mending what winter ruined.
What I can't get over is something simple, easy:
How could a dandelion seed head seemingly
grow overnight? A neighbor mows the lawn
and bam, the next morning, there's a hundred
dandelion seed heads straight as arrows
and proud as cats high above any green blade
of manicured grass. It must bug some folks,
a flower so tricky it can reproduce asexually,
making perfect identical selves, bam, another me,
bam, another me. I can't help it—I root
for that persecuted rosette so hyper in its
own making it seems to devour the land.
Even its name, translated from the French
dent de lion, means lion's tooth. It's vicious,
made for a time that requires tenacity, a way
of remaking the toughest self while everyone
else is asleep.

DREAM OF THE RAVEN

When the ten-speed, lightweight bicycle broke down
off the highway lined thick with orange trees, I noticed
a giant raven's head protruding from the waxy leaves.
The bird was stuck somehow, mangled in the branches,
crying out. Wide-eyed, I held the bird's face close to mine.
Beak to nose. Dark brown iris to dark brown iris. Feather
to feather. This was not the Chihuahuan raven or the fan-
tailed raven or the common raven. Nothing was common
about the way we stared at one another while a stranger
untangled the bird's claws from the tree's limbs and he, finally
free, became a naked child swinging in the wind.

THE VISITOR

A neighborhood tuxedo cat's walking the fence line
and the dogs are going bonkers in the early morning.
The louder they bark, the more their vexation grows,
the less the cat seems to care. She's behind my raised
beds now, no doubt looking for the family of field mice
I've been leaving be because why not? The cat's
dressed up for this occasion of trespass, formal
attire for the canine taunting, but the whole clamor
is making me uneasy. This might be what growing
older is. My problem: I see all the angles of what
could go wrong so I never know what side to be on.
Save the mice, shoo the cat, quiet the dogs? Let
the cat have at it? Let the dogs have at it? Instead,
I do what I do best: nothing. I watch the cat
leap into the drainage ditch, dew-wet fur against
the daylilies, and disappear. The dogs go quiet
again, and the mice are safe in their caves, and
I'm here waiting for something to happen to me.

LATE SUMMER AFTER A PANIC ATTACK

I can't undress from the pressure of leaves,
the lobed edges leaning toward the window
like an unwanted male gaze on the backside
(they wish to bless and bless and hush).
What if I want to go devil instead? Bow
down to the madness that makes me. Drone
of the neighbor's mowing, a red mailbox flag
erected, a dog bark from three houses over,
and this is what a day is. Beetle on the wainscoting,
dead branch breaking but not breaking, stones
from the sea next to stones from the river,
unanswered messages like ghosts in the throat,
a siren whining high toward town repeating
that the emergency is not here, repeating
that this loud silence is only where you live.

BUST

I'm driving alone in the predawn
dark to the airport, nerves nearly gone
when I fly now, gravity only another holy
thing to contend with, what pushes us
down squeezing out the body's air.
The shock jock's morning jawing clangs
in its exaggerated American male register
to tell us how the twenty-four-year-old Colombian
woman whose breasts had been hacked
open and stuffed with one kilogram
of cocaine swiftly admitted the smuggled
property because she was in dire agony.
Wounds rupturing, raging infection,
she was rushed to a Berlin hospital.
Her three kids were home in her country
where she worked in agriculture, another
word for cultivation of land, for making
something out of dirt. The rude radio
disc jockey licks his lips into the studio's mic
and says something about motorboating
her tits jammed with nose candy and I'm
thinking of my friend who's considering
a mastectomy to stay alive, another who
said she'd cut them off herself if it meant
living. Passport and boots that slip on and off,
a sleepy stream through the radiation
machine. A passive pat-down of my outline
and I'm heading somewhere else before
the world has even woken up. I've got shit
to do and I need to lose a little weight before

I turn older. There's the email scan of the bank
statement showing barely enough, the IRS
check, the dentist that'll have to wait until
payday next month. We do what we have
to do to not cleave the body too quickly.
I wait for my zone to be called and line
up with all the others, the woman's voice
over the intercom's buzz reminding us
the flight is full, reminding us to carry
only what we need. The chill rises
up in the jet bridge as does the tremor
in my chest as we board, this shiver of need
that moves my hand to my breastbone,
some small gesture of tenderness for this
masterpiece of anatomy I cling to.

DEAD STARS

Out here, there's a bowing even the trees are doing.
        Winter's icy hand at the back of all of us.
Black bark, slick yellow leaves, a kind of stillness that feels
so mute it's almost in another year.

I am a hearth of spiders these days: a nest of trying.

We point out the stars that make Orion as we take out
        the trash, the rolling containers a song of suburban thunder.

It's almost romantic as we adjust the waxy blue
        recycling bin until you say, *Man, we should really learn
some new constellations.*

And it's true. We keep forgetting about Antlia, Centaurus,
        Draco, Lacerta, Hydra, Lyra, Lynx.

But mostly we're forgetting we're dead stars too, my mouth is full
        of dust and I wish to reclaim the rising—

to lean in the spotlight of streetlight with you, toward
        what's larger within us, toward how we were born.

Look, we are not unspectacular things.
        We've come this far, survived this much. What

would happen if we decided to survive more? To love harder?

What if we stood up with our synapses and flesh and said, *No.
        No*, to the rising tides.

Stood for the many mute mouths of the sea, of the land?

What would happen if we used our bodies to bargain

for the safety of others, for earth,
        if we declared a clean night, if we stopped being terrified,

if we launched our demands into the sky, made ourselves so big
people could point to us with the arrows they make in their minds,

rolling their trash bins out, after all of this is over?

DREAM OF DESTRUCTION

We somehow knew the electric orange volcanic ooze
of hot lava was bound to bury us all, little spurts of ash
popping early like precum and not innocuous at all
blasted into the sky like a warning siren on the horizon.
The air felt different. The sky felt different. You felt different.
Still, there I was down in the valley where I was born, coyotes
on the ridges of the Mayacamas, turning over the steamy earth
to plant a garden. You were standing on the steps, staring
out at the sky's ominous openings, a mouth of terrible red,
like a tongue that'd been bitten so often it was not a tongue
but a bloody wound with which the earth tried to speak. I held
that black rake in my hand like a weapon. I was going to rake
until that goddamn lava came and killed us. I was going
to rake and rake and rake, feverishly and mean, until the fertile
dirt knew I was willing to die trying.

PREY

The muffled, ruptured voice of a friend
turns into an electrical signal and breaks open
to tell me her sister has died. A muted pause,
then a heaving. Sounds sucked from lungs.
Outside, as the sun descends to inch-high
on the fallow horizon, a hawk grasp-lands
on the telephone pole. Brawny and barrel-
chested, it perches eyeing the late winter
seed head of switchgrass. Later, we're talking
about self-care, being strong, surviving
a long time. The hawk launches as the sun
oozes puce and ochre and sinks. I write
to another friend who says her partner
is like a hawk—steadfast, wary. I think
of the sharp-shinned hunters, the Cooper's,
the Swainson's, how hawks are both serene
and scary as hell, scary that is, if you're
the mouse. That's the trick, we say,
isn't it? Don't be the mouse.

2

THE BURYING BEETLE

I like to imagine even the plants
want attention, so I weed for four
hours straight, assuring the tomatoes
feel July's hot breath on the neck,
the Japanese maple can stretch,
the sweet potatoes, the spider plants,
the Asiatic lilies can flourish in this
place we've dared to say we "own."
Each nicked spindle of morning glory
or kudzu or purslane or yellow rocket
(*Barbarea vulgaris* for Christ's sake),
and I find myself missing everyone I know.
I don't know why. First come the piles
of nutsedge and creeper and then an
ache that fills the skin like the *Cercospora*
blight that's killing the blue skyrocket juniper
slowly from the inside out. Sure, I know
what it is to be lonely, but today's special
is a physical need to be touched by someone
decent, a pulsing palm to the back. My man
is in South Africa still, and people just keep
dying even when I try to pretend like they're
not. The crown vetch and the curly dock
are almost eliminated as I survey the neatness
of my work. I don't feel I deserve this time,
or the small plot of earth I get to mold into
someplace livable. I lost God awhile ago.
And I don't want to pray, but I can picture
the plants deepening right now into the soil,
wanting to live, so I lie down among them,

in my ripped pink tank top, filthy and covered
in sweat, among red burying beetles and dirt
that's been turned and turned like a problem
in the mind.

HOW WE ARE MADE

For Philip Levine

For months, I was a cannonball
dropped down the bore, reeling
in blurry vomitous swirls toward
the fuse; forty days with vertigo
is like that. My new equilibrium
was spinning inside the chambers
of spherical blackness when the news
came. You, with your wiry limbs
of hard verse, inky gap-toothed grin
of gristle and work, you who grimly
told us to stop messing around,
to make this survival matter
like a factory line, like fish scaling,
like filament and rubble, you
who would say, most likely,
this was all sentimental crap, you
had gone to cinders, blasted
into the ether without so much
as smoke. I stood then on the icy hill
under the expressway, filled
with the salt you had given me,
and for the first time that year,
my entire world stood still.

THE LIGHT THE LIVING SEE

For Adam & Michael

We're stopped in Subiaco
   to lay stones on stone
      at a fellow penner's grave

where we jaw, punchdrunk
   and carsick, about being buried
      or burned up. *I don't want*

to take up any more space,
   I tell the boys, both fathers now,
      who, shaped like trees, lean

toward the earth. I imagine
   their old daughters leaving a slice
      of gas station moon pie,

rye, a nickel-plated acorn, ladies
   picnicking in the shade of a pine
      as immobile as the body's husk.

Chemicals and maggots, sure,
   but also a place to grieve, a creek,
      a constellation of death to count on.

These men know something
   I don't. That someone will grieve
      past their bones, count on them

to be there among the shaded trunks
   of pines like the stark bars
      of a generous cage.

(What if no one comes to the cliffside
   where my skin's ashes set sail?
      No mourning kin, no lost hitchhiker.)

But friends, it's lunchtime,
   and doesn't my mouth still work;
      my appetite, my forked tongue?

THE DEAD BOY

It was spring then too, and the Southern grass
was thick with ant legs and needling beetles.
The day was all lemonade and meditation
on the true-blue atmosphere that held me
in the palm of quietude and survival. But,
from the summer-thinned dorm rooms, a young
woman came running, her oversized T-shirt
billowing, her straight brown hair wild as she
begged us to call 9-1-1. Because we were
the adults, Fred and I ran toward the stale
hollow room where, already purple with death's
permanent hue, the boy was gone. But Fred,
being a father, and maybe more hopeful,
tried to revive him. So I tried too. Turned
him to see the ruined face like a petaled
jellyfish washed to the stormy shore.
I don't want to admit this, but I hated
him. Hated his face that I already knew
I'd see forever, hated the needle on the waxy
dorm room desk, hated the dorm, hated
the kid I loved back in college who mainlined
until his too-high pal had a seizure, hated
my ex who had died that way a different spring.
I hated the world, the pain of it that circles in us,
that makes us want to be the moon,
the treasure, and not the thing on the sea
floor. Later, I found out his name was Griffin,
part lion, part eagle, named for the king
of the creatures, named the guardian
of riches. And because symbols matter, I try

to say his name: Griffin, Griffin, but because
language matters too, I have to tell you: I did not
feel like I was laying down a lion, or a king,
or an eagle, but a poor suffering son, and even
if I hate these words and the drug that dragged
him there, he is etched in my mind, named
in language forever and only as: dead boy,
dead boy, and gone.

WHAT I WANT TO REMEMBER

Right before General Vallejo's home,
with its stately stone and yellow walls,

there's a field along the footpath
where spring rains bring the frogs,

a whole symphony of them, breaking
open the hours just after the sun

sinks into the Pacific Ocean only
an hour away. Why am I placing

you here? I'm on a plane going west
and all the humans are so loud

it hurts the blood. But once I sat
next to a path that was still warm

from the day's heat, cross-legged
with my friend named Echo who taught

me how to amplify the strange sound
the frogs made by cupping my ears.

I need to hold this close within me,
when today's news is full of dead children,

their faces opening their mouths for air
that will not come. Once I was a child too

and my friend and I sat for maybe an hour,
eyes adjusting to the night sky, cupping

and uncupping our ears to hear
the song the tenderest animals made.

OVERPASS

The road wasn't as hazardous then,
when I'd walk to the steel guardrail,
lean my bendy girl body over, and stare
at the cold creek water. In a wet spring,
the water'd run clear and high, minnows
mouthing the sand and silt, a crawdad
shadowed by the shore's long reeds.
I could stare for hours, something
always new in each watery wedge—
a bottle top, a man's black boot, a toad.
Once, a raccoon's carcass, half under
the overpass, half out, slowly decayed
over months. I'd check on him each day,
watching until the white bones of his hand
were totally skinless and seemed to reach
out toward the sun as it hit the water,
showing all five of his sweet tensile fingers
still clinging. I don't think I worshipped
him, his deadness, but I liked the evidence
of him, how it felt like a job to daily
take note of his shifting into the sand.

THE MILLIONTH DREAM OF YOUR RETURN

At the tequila tasting bar called Izquierda Iguana
where the silvery agave plants were pure hydroponic
and upside down so you had to swerve around them
to get served, I suddenly remembered you were coming
in that evening, a special return. I rushed to the cavernous loft
where the power was all on one ancient grid so the lights
flickered each time someone opened the refrigerator,
and put on the white dress that you had once said made you look
like an angel with its real swan feathers and fool's gold.
Then I sat for a long time in the night and waited. At dawn,
I woke with feathers sticky on my tongue and I remembered
you were dead all over again.

BALD EAGLES IN A FIELD

She was almost gone at that point,
enough so we could start to make plans.

Bright for a February near Fishtown,
Skagit Bay another sun on the earth

shining upward. On our way for groceries,
we saw one eagle in a field, then another.

I had never seen two bald eagles together
like that, and it felt like a sign, something

that would shift things forever, but it wasn't
really, it was just a moment, dad and daughter

pulled over in the car, silent and breathing
for a singular instance before all we knew

took flight.

I'M SURE ABOUT MAGIC

After the artist Dario Robleto

With dust from every bone in the body,
and the strange material trinitite (a glass
forged in the heat of the 1945 atomic blasts),
the artist makes a spell for the dead. Me?
I cross the wide river the same color as trees,
thinking what could I excavate, melt, smash
of yours. The copper pots you bought to last
turned into a heavy necklace for all to see
like Cleopatra and her beloved Caesar coins,
late August, hot, overripe trailing black
dewberries cooked into an inky purple stain
for a tattoo on the wrist, juniper-laden cold gin
mixed with beeswax and lit from a stolen match
all wasted like your too-short life down the drain.

WONDER WOMAN

Standing at the swell of the muddy Mississippi
after the urgent care doctor had just said, *Well,*
sometimes shit happens, I fell fast and hard
for New Orleans all over again. Pain pills swirled
in the purse along with a spell for later. It's taken
a while for me to admit, I am in a raging battle
with my body, a spinal column thirty-five degrees
bent, vertigo that comes and goes like a DC Comics
villain nobody can kill. Invisible pain is both
a blessing and a curse. *You always look so happy,*
said a stranger once as I shifted to my good side
grinning. But that day, alone on the riverbank,
brass blaring from the Steamboat Natchez,
out of the corner of my eye, I saw a girl, maybe half my age,
dressed, for no apparent reason, as Wonder Woman.
She strutted by in all her strength and glory, invincible,
eternal, and when I stood to clap (because who wouldn't have),
she bowed and posed like she knew I needed a myth—
a woman, by a river, indestructible.

THE REAL REASON

I don't have any tattoos is not my story to tell. It's my
mother's. Once, walking down Bedford Avenue in my twenties,

I called her as I did, as I do. I told her how I wanted a tattoo
on the back of my neck. Something minor, but permanent,

and she is an artist, I wanted her to create the design, a symbol,
a fish I dream of every night. An underwater talisman, a mother's

gift on my body. To be clear, I thought she'd be honored. But do we
ever really know each other fully? A silence like a hospital room; she

was in tears. I swore then that I wouldn't get one. Wouldn't let a needle
touch my neck, my arm, my torso. I'd stay me, my skin the skin

she welcomed me into the world with. It wasn't until later that
I knew it wasn't so much the tattoo, but the marking, the idea

of scars. What you don't know (and this is why this is not my story)
is that my mother is scarred from burns over a great deal of her body.

Most from an explosion that took her first child she was carrying
in her belly, others from the skin grafts where they took skin to cover

what needed it. She was in her late twenties when that happened.
Outside her studio in the center of town. You have to understand,

my mother is beautiful. Tall and elegant, thin and strong. I have not
known her any other way, her skin that I mapped with my young

fingers, its strange hardness in places, its patterns like quilts here,
riverbeds there. She's wondrous, preternatural, survived fire,

the ending of an unborn child. Heat and flame and death, all made
her into something seemingly magical, a phoenixess. What I know

now is she wanted something else for me. For me to wake each
morning and recognize my own flesh, for this one thing she made—

me—to remain how she intended, for one of us
to make it out unscathed.

THE YEAR OF THE GOLDFINCHES

There were two that hung and hovered
by the mud puddle and the musk thistle.
Flitting from one splintered fence post
to another, bathing in the rainwater's glint
like it was a mirror to some other universe
where things were more acceptable, easier
than the place I lived. I'd watch for them:
the bright peacocking male, the low-watt
female, on each morning walk, days spent
digging for some sort of elusive answer
to the question my curving figure made.
Later, I learned that they were a symbol
of resurrection. Of course they were,
my two yellow-winged twins feasting
on thorns and liking it.

NOTES ON THE BELOW

For Mammoth Cave National Park

Tell me—humongous cavern, tell me, wet limestone, sandstone
caprock, bat-wing, sightless translucent cave shrimp,

this endless plummet into more of the unknown,
              tell me how one keeps secrets for so long.

All my life, I've lived above the ground,
              car wheels over paved roads, roots breaking through concrete,
and still I've not understood the reel of this life's purpose.

Not so much living, but a hovering without sense.

What's it like to be always night? No moon, but a few lit-up
              circles at your many openings. Endless dark, still time
must enter you. Like a train, like a green river?

Tell me what it is to be the thing rooted in shadow.
       To be the thing not touched by light (no, that's not it)—
to not even need the light? I envy; I envy that.

Desire is a tricky thing, the boiling of the body's wants,
              more praise, more hands holding the knives away.

I've been the one who has craved and craved until I could not see
       beyond my own greed. There's a whole nation of us.

To forgive myself, I point to the earth as witness.

To you, your Frozen Niagara, your Fat Man's Misery,
        you with your 400 miles of interlocking caves that lead
only to more of you, tell me

what it is to be quiet, and yet still breathing.

        Ruler of the Underlying, let me
speak to both the dead and the living as you do. Speak
to the ruined earth, the stalactites, the eastern small-footed bat,

to honor this: the length of days. To speak to the core
    that creates and swallows, to speak not always to what's
shouting, but to what's underneath asking for nothing.

I am at the mouth of the cave. I am willing to crawl.

SUNDOWN & ALL THE DAMAGE DONE

Nearly nine and still the sun's not slunk
into its nightly digs. The burnt-meat smell
of midweek cookouts and wet grass
hangs in the air like loose familiar summer
garb. Standing by the magnolia tree, I think
if I were to live as long as she did, I'd have
eleven more years. And if I were to live as long
as him, I'd have forty-nine. As long as him,
I'd be dead already. As long as her, this
would be my final year. There's a strange
contentment to this countdown, a nodding
to this time, where I get to stand under
the waxy leaves of the ancient genus, a tree
that appeared before even the bees, and
watch as fireflies land on the tough tepals
until each broad flower glows like a torchlit
mausoleum. They call the beetle's conspicuous
bioluminescence "a cold light," but why then
do I still feel so much fire?

ON A LAMPPOST LONG AGO

I don't know what to think of first
        in the list

of all the things that are disappearing: fishes, birds, trees, flowers, bees,

and languages too. They say that if historical rates are averaged,
        a language will die every four months.

In the time it takes to say *I love you*, or move in with someone,
or admit to the child you're carrying, all the intricate words
of a language become extinct.

There are too many things to hold in the palm of the brain.
Your father with Alzheimer's uses the word *thing* to describe
many different nouns and we guess the word he means.
When we get it right, he nods as if it's obvious.

When we get it wrong, his face closes like a fist.

Out walking in the neighborhood, there's a wide metal lamppost
        that has scratched into it "Brandy Earlywine loves
Jack Pickett" and then there come the hearts. The barrage of hearts
scratched over and over as if, just in case we have forgotten

the word *love*, we will know its symbol. As if Miss Earlywine
wanted us to know that—even after she and Mr. Pickett

have passed on, their real hearts stopped, the ones that don't look
anything like those little symbols—they frantically, furiously,

late one night under the streetlight while their parents thought
they were asleep, inscribed onto the body of something like
a permanent tree, a heart—so that even after their bodies

have ceased to be bodies, their mouths no longer capable of words,
that universal shape will tell you how she felt, one blue evening,
long ago, when there were still 7,000 languages that named and honored

the plants and animals each in their
                own way, when your father said *thing* and we knew what it meant,
and the bees were big and round and buzzing.

OF ROOTS & ROAMERS

Have you ever noticed how the trees
change from state to state? Not all
at once, of course, more like a weaver
gradually weaving in another color
until the old trees become scarce
and new trees offer a shaded kingdom
all their own. Before I knew the names
of towns or roads, I could recognize
places by the trees: Northern California's
smooth-skinned madrone, looming eucalyptus,
fuzzy fragrant flowers of the acacia. So
much of America belongs to the trees.
Even when we can't agree on much,
there's still the man returning from his
late shift at the local bar, who takes
a long look at the bird's nest in the maple,
pats the trunk like a friend's forearm,
mumbles something about staying safe,
and returns home. And the girl whose
slapdash tree fort we can see from our blurry
window, how she stands there to wave
at a world she does not even know
the half of yet. My grandmother once
complained she couldn't see much
of America on her cross-country trip because
it was all just trees. Ask her, she'll laugh as she
tells you. Still, without the bother of licenses
or attention to a state line, a border, they
just grow where they've grown all their lives:
there, a small stand of white pine arrives,

there, a redwood begins to show itself along
the coastline, water oaks in the south, willows.
Their power is in not moving, so we must
move to them.

KILLING METHODS

Outside, after grieving for days,
I'm thinking of how we make stories,
pluck them like beetles out of the air,

collect them, pin their glossy backs
to the board like the rows of stolen
beauties, dead, displayed at Isla Negra,

where the waves broke over us
and I still loved the country, wanted
to suck the bones of the buried.

Now, I'm outside a normal house
while friends cook and please
and pour secrets into each other.

A crow pierces the sky, ominous,
clanging like an alarm, but there
is no ocean here, just tap water

rising in the sink, a sadness clean
of history only because it's new,
a few weeks old, our national wound.

I don't know how to hold this truth,
so I kill it, pin its terrible wings down
in case, later, no one believes me.

FULL GALLOP

The night after, I dream I chop
all the penises off, the ones that
keep coming through the walls.

Tied in sweat-wet sheets, I wake
aching, how I've longed for touch
for so much of my bodied time.

In the shower later, I notice new
layers I've grown, softness love tosses
you after years of streetlights alone.

I will never harm you, your brilliant
skin I rub against in the night,
still, part of me is haunted—

a shadow baying inside me
who wants to snap her hind leg
back, buck the rider, follow

that fugitive call into oblivion.

DREAM OF THE MEN

At the beach that was so gray it seemed stone—
gray water, gray sky, gray blanket, and the wind
some sort of gray perpetual motion machine—
we gathered like a blustery coven on the blanket
from Mexico woven with white and gray threads
into a pattern of owls and great seabirds. Then,
they came: the men. Blankets full of them, talking,
talking, talking, talking, and our mouths were sewn
shut with patient smiles while they talked about
the country where they were from; their hands
like slick seaweed were everywhere, unwelcome,
multicellular, touching us.

A NEW NATIONAL ANTHEM

The truth is, I've never cared for the National
Anthem. If you think about it, it's not a good
song. Too high for most of us with "the rockets'
red glare" and then there are the bombs.
(Always, always there is war and bombs.)
Once, I sang it at homecoming and threw
even the tenacious high school band off key.
But the song didn't mean anything, just a call
to the field, something to get through before
the pummeling of youth. And what of the stanzas
we never sing, the third that mentions "no refuge
could save the hireling and the slave"? Perhaps
the truth is every song of this country
has an unsung third stanza, something brutal
snaking underneath us as we blindly sing
the high notes with a beer sloshing in the stands
hoping our team wins. Don't get me wrong, I do
like the flag, how it undulates in the wind
like water, elemental, and best when it's humbled,
brought to its knees, clung to by someone who
has lost everything, when it's not a weapon,
when it flickers, when it folds up so perfectly
you can keep it until it's needed, until you can
love it again, until the song in your mouth feels
like sustenance, a song where the notes are sung
by even the ageless woods, the shortgrass plains,
the Red River Gorge, the fistful of land left
unpoisoned, that song that's our birthright,
that's sung in silence when it's too hard to go on,
that sounds like someone's rough fingers weaving

into another's, that sounds like a match being lit
in an endless cave, the song that says my bones
are your bones, and your bones are my bones,
and isn't that enough?

CARGO

I wish I could write to you from underwater,
      the warm bath covering my ears—
one of which has three marks in the exact
shape of a triangle, my own atmosphere's asterism.

Last night, the fire engine sirens were so loud
they drowned out even the constant bluster
      of the inbound freight trains. Did I tell you,
the R. J. Corman Railroad runs 500 feet from us?

Before everything shifted and I aged into this body,
  my grandparents lived above San Timoteo Canyon
where the Southern Pacific Railroad roared each scorching
California summer day. I'd watch for the trains,
howling as they came.

Manuel is in Chicago today, and we've both admitted
    that we're traveling with our passports now.
Reports of ICE raids and both of our bloods
are requiring new medication.

I wish we could go back to the windy dock,
drinking pink wine and talking smack.
Now, it's gray and pitchfork.

The supermarket here is full of grass seed like spring
      might actually come, but I don't know. And you?

I heard from a friend that you're still working on saving
          words. All I've been working on is napping, and maybe
being kinder to others, to myself.

Just this morning, I saw seven cardinals brash and bold
          as sin in a leafless tree. I let them be for a long while before
I shook the air and screwed it all up just by being alive too.

Am I braver than those birds?

Do you ever wonder what the trains carry? Aluminum ingots,
          plastic, brick, corn syrup, limestone, fury, alcohol, joy.

All the world is moving, even sand from one shore to another
is being shuttled. I live my life half afraid, and half shouting
at the trains when they thunder by. This letter to you is both.

THE CONTRACT SAYS: WE'D LIKE THE CONVERSATION TO BE BILINGUAL

When you come, bring your brown-
ness so we can be sure to please

the funders. Will you check this
box; we're applying for a grant.

Do you have any poems that speak
to troubled teens? Bilingual is best.

Would you like to come to dinner
with the patrons and sip Patrón?

Will you tell us the stories that make
us uncomfortable, but not complicit?

Don't read us the one where you
are just like us. Born to a green house,

garden, don't tell us how you picked
tomatoes and ate them in the dirt

watching vultures pick apart another
bird's bones in the road. Tell us the one

about your father stealing hubcaps
after a colleague said that's what his

kind did. Tell us how he came
to the meeting wearing a poncho

and tried to sell the man his hubcaps
back. Don't mention your father

was a teacher, spoke English, loved
making beer, loved baseball, tell us

again about the poncho, the hubcaps,
how he stole them, how he did the thing

he was trying to prove he didn't do.

IT'S HARDER

Not to unravel the intentions of the other—
the slight gesture over the coffee table, a raised
eyebrow at the passing minuscule skirt, a wick
snuffed out at the evening's end, a sympathetic
nod, a black garbage can rolled out so slowly
he hovers there, outside, alone, a little longer,
the child's thieving fingers, the face that's serene
as cornfields, the mouth screwed into a plum,
the way I can't remember which blue lake
has the whole train underneath its surface,
so now, every blue lake has a whole train
underneath its surface.

3

AGAINST BELONGING

It's been six years since we moved here, green
of the tall grasses outstretched like fingers waving.
I remember the first drive in; the American beech,
sassafras, chestnut oak, yellow birch were just
plain trees back then. I didn't know we'd stay long.
I missed the Sonoma coast line, the winding
roads that opened onto places called Goat Rock,
Furlong Gulch, Salmon Creek. Once, when I was
young, we camped out at Russian Gulch and learned
the names of all the grasses, the tide pool animals,
the creatures of the redwoods, properly identifying
seemed more important than science, more like
creation. With each new name, the world expanded.
I give names to everything now because it makes
me feel useful. Currently, three snakes surround our
house. One in front, one near the fire pit, and one
near the raised beds of beets and carrots. Harmless
Eastern garter snakes, small, but ever expanding.
I check on them each day, watch their round eyes
blink in the sun that fuels them. I've named them
so no one is tempted to kill them (a way of offering
reprieve, tenderness). But sometimes I feel them
moving around inside me, the three snakes hissing—
what cannot be tamed, what shakes off citizenship,
what draws her own signature with her body
in whatever dirt she wants.

INSTRUCTIONS ON NOT GIVING UP

More than the fuchsia funnels breaking out
of the crabapple tree, more than the neighbor's
almost obscene display of cherry limbs shoving
their cotton candy–colored blossoms to the slate
sky of spring rains, it's the greening of the trees
that really gets to me. When all the shock of white
and taffy, the world's baubles and trinkets, leave
the pavement strewn with the confetti of aftermath,
the leaves come. Patient, plodding, a green skin
growing over whatever winter did to us, a return
to the strange idea of continuous living despite
the mess of us, the hurt, the empty. Fine then,
I'll take it, the tree seems to say, a new slick leaf
unfurling like a fist, I'll take it all.

WOULD YOU RATHER

Remember that car ride to Sea-Tac, how your sister's kids
played a frenzied game of *Would You Rather*, where each choice

ticktocked between superpowers or towering piles of a food
too often denied, *Would You Rather*

have fiery lasers that shoot out of your eyes,
or eat sundaes with whip cream for every meal?

We dealt it out quick,
        without stopping to check ourselves for the truth.

We played so hard that I got good at the questions, learned
                there had to be an equality

to each weighted ask. Now I'm an expert at comparing things
that give the illusion they equal each other.

You said our Plan B was just to live our lives:
more time, more sleep, travel—

            and still I'm making a list of all the places
I found out I wasn't carrying a child.

At the outdoor market in San Telmo, Isla Negra's wide iris of sea,

the baseball stadium, the supermarket,
the Muhammad Ali museum, but always

the last time tops the list, in the middle of the Golden Gate Bridge,
looking over toward Alcatraz, a place they should burn and redeliver

to the gulls and cormorants, common daisies and seagrass.

Down below the girder that's still not screened against jumpers,
so that it seems almost like a dare, an invitation,

we watched a seal make a sinuous shimmy in the bay.

Would you rather? Would I rather?
The game is endless and without a winner.

Do you remember how the seal was so far under
the deafening sound of traffic, the whir of wind mixed
with car horns and gasoline, such a small

speck of black movement alone in the churning waves
between rock and shore?

Didn't she seem happy?

MAYBE I'LL BE ANOTHER KIND OF MOTHER

Snow today, a layer outlining the maple like a halo,
or rather, a fungus. So many sharp edges in the month.

I'm thinking I'll never sit down at the table
at the restaurant, you know that one, by the window?

Women gathered in paisley scarves with rusty iced tea,
talking about their kids, their little time-suckers,

how their mouths want so much, a gesture of exhaustion,
a roll of the eyes, *But I wouldn't have it any other way,*

their bags full of crayons and nut-free snacks, the light
coming in the window, a small tear of joy melting like ice.

No, I'll be elsewhere, having spent all day writing words
and then at the movies, where my man bought me a drink,

because our bodies are our own, and what will it be?
A blockbuster? A man somewhere saving the world, alone,

with only the thought of his family to get him through.
The film will be forgettable, a thin star in a blurred sea of stars,

I'll come home and rub my whole face against my dog's
belly; she'll be warm and want to sleep some more.

I'll stare at the tree and the ice will have melted, so
it's only the original tree again, green branches giving way

to other green branches, everything coming back to life.

CARRYING

The sky's white with November's teeth,
and the air is ash and woodsmoke.
A flush of color from the dying tree,
a cargo train speeding through, and there,
that's me, standing in the wintering
grass watching the dog suffer the cold
leaves. I'm not large from this distance,
just a fence post, a hedge of holly.
Wider still, beyond the rumble of overpass,
mares look for what's left of green
in the pasture, a few weanlings kick
out, and theirs is the same sky, white
like a calm flag of surrender pulled taut.
A few farms over, there's our mare,
her belly barrel-round with foal, or idea
of foal. It's Kentucky, late fall, and any
mare worth her salt is carrying the next
potential stakes winner. Ours, her coat
thicker with the season's muck, leans against
the black fence and this image is heavy
within me. How my own body, empty,
clean of secrets, knows how to carry her,
knows we were all meant for something.

WHAT I DIDN'T KNOW BEFORE

was how horses simply give birth to other
horses. Not a baby by any means, not
a creature of liminal spaces, but already
a four-legged beast hellbent on walking,
scrambling after the mother. A horse gives way
to another horse and then suddenly there are
two horses, just like that. That's how I loved you.
You, off the long train from Red Bank carrying
a coffee as big as your arm, a bag with two
computers swinging in it unwieldily at your
side. I remember we broke into laughter
when we saw each other. What was between
us wasn't a fragile thing to be coddled, cooed
over. It came out fully formed, ready to run.

MASTERING

I'm in Texas at a bar with a friend who doesn't drink
        anymore and I've missed him. We order food and share
and talk aging bodies and Mexico and how the mind goes mad.

We talk about a friend who's going blind, the pressure
        on his brain, how much we admire his fierce allegiance
to this world, his unflagging wail into the abyss.

I like being at this bar with a man I admire
        but don't love, don't need to fleece for affection. It makes
me feel all grown up, like I should get a good-job chip too.

We talk about marriage and the tender skin
        of the other. I lay out the plans for my upcoming
wedding—a mountain named after the moon,
blooms in my hair, my beloved.

We've known each other almost fifteen years, my friend
        with eyes the color of a clear cenote. I trust him. He leans in,

tells me the real miracle, more than marriage, the thing that makes you
believe there might be a god after all, is the making of a child.

He stares at me, but I am not there anymore. I don't say
        we've tried a long time, been sad, been happy,
that perhaps the only thing I can make

is love and art. I want to tell him that's enough. Isn't it? Isn't love
that doesn't result in a seed, a needy body, another suckling animal,

still love? Isn't that supernatural? Screw your god. He's showing
        me a photo now of his child and I'm unfolding and folding
the napkin. He's pointing out how amazing his child is. I order

a drink because I can. (And maybe because he can't.) He retreats
        in his seat. I take a long sip and really look into his eyes.

I want him to notice what he said, how a woman might feel agony,
emptiness, how he's lucky it's me he said it to because I won't
        vaporize him. I sip again, I want him to see how much pleasure

I can handle, my tongue a tuning fork, how mute and mirror I can be,
even with these ordinary wonders he can't see swirling around us.

THE LAST THING

First there was the blue wing
of a scraggly loud jay tucked
into the shrubs. Then the bluish-
black moth drunkenly tripping
from blade to blade. Then
the quiet that came roaring
in like the R. J. Corman over
Broadway near the RV shop.
These are the last three things
that happened. Not in the universe,
but here, in the basin of my mind,
where I'm always making a list
for you, recording the day's minor
urchins: silvery dust mote, pistachio
shell, the dog eating a sugar
snap pea. It's going to rain soon,
close clouds bloated above us,
the air like a net about to release
all the caught fishes, a storm
siren in the distance. I know
you don't always understand,
but let me point to the first
wet drops landing on the stones,
the noise like fingers drumming
the skin. I can't help it. I will
never get over making everything
such a big deal.

LOVE POEM WITH APOLOGIES FOR MY APPEARANCE

Sometimes, I think you get the worst
of me. The much-loved loose forest-green
sweatpants, the long bra-less days, hair
knotted and uncivilized, a shadowed brow
where the devilish thoughts do their hoofed
dance on the brain. I'd like to say this means
I love you, the stained white cotton T-shirt,
the tears, pistachio shells, the mess of orange
peels on my desk, but it's different than that.
I move in this house with you, the way I move
in my mind, unencumbered by beauty's cage.
I do like I do in the tall grass, more animal-me
than much else. I'm wrong, it is that I love you,
but it's more that when you say it back, lights
out, a cold wind through curtains, for maybe
the first time in my life, I believe it.

SWAY

What is it about words that make the world
        fit easier? Air and time.

Since last we spoke, I've been better.
I slept again once the Pink Moon
        moved off a little, put her pants back on, let me be.

Are you sleeping again?

I'm home in the bluegrass now, one of the places
my body feels at ease. I can't stop
        putting plants in the ground. There's a hunger in me,

a need to watch something grow. A neighbor brought me
five new hostas to plant along the fence line that's shaded all afternoon.

As I dug into the ground making room around the maple,
I found a bunch of wild strawberries, flowering.
I let them be: the heart berry. Red,

like our rage. The red of your desert. Your heart too.

My neighbor and her wife bring me plants and chive pesto
        and we let our dogs run under the fence
to multiply their space. Small beasts running in more air.

I have been alone a long time this year.

She says when she looks at me, she is reminded of time.

I didn't know what she meant, so she repeated,
When I see you, I become very aware of time.

A grackle, now two, are joining us here, in the vines; they're
too heavy for the young spring branches.

My man is coming home today, driving ten hours
to be home, and by god, I will throw my body toward him,

the way you wrote: *How is it that we know what we are?*

Maybe this letter is to say, if it is red where you are,
know there is also green, the serrated leaves of dandelion, lemon balm,
purple sage, peppermint, a small plum tree by the shed.

I don't know how to make medicine, or cure what's scarring
this planet, but I know that last night, the train came roaring

right as I needed it. I was alone and I was time, but
the train made a noise so I would listen. I was standing so

close, a body on a bridge, so that I could feel how
the air shifted to make room for the train. How it's easier

if we become more like a body of air, branches, and make room
for this red charging thing that barrels through us,

how afterward our leaves shake and stand straighter.

SACRED OBJECTS

I'm driving down to Tennessee, but before I get there, I stop at the Kentucky state line to fuel up and pee. The dog's in the car and the weather's fine. As I pump the gas a man in his black Ford F-150 yells out his window about my body. I actually can't remember what it was. Nice tits. Nice ass. Something I've been hearing my whole life. Except sometimes it's not *Nice ass*, it's *Big ass* or something a bit more cruel. I pretend not to hear him. I pretend my sunglasses hide my whole body. Right then, a man with black hair, who could be an uncle of mine, pulls by in his truck and nods. He's towing a trailer that's painted gray with white letters. The letters read: *Sacred Objects*. I imagine a trailer full of Las Vírgenes de Guadalupe—concrete, marble, or wood—all wobbly from their travels. All of these female statues hidden together in this secret shadowed spot on their way to find a place where they'll be safe, even worshipped, or at the very least allowed to live in the light.

SOMETIMES I THINK MY BODY LEAVES A SHAPE IN THE AIR

I slipped my hands in the cold salt froth
        of the Pacific Ocean just two days ago. Planetlike
and everything aquatic, even the sky, where an eagle
unfolded so much larger than my shadow.

I was struck translucent. A good look for me!

My hands were slick with the water I was born next to,
        and there was a whole hour that I felt lived in, like a room.

I wish to be untethered and tethered all at once, my skin
        singes the sheets and there's a tremor in the marrow.

On the way back to the city, a sign read:
"Boneless, Heartless, Binge-Worthy."
        Next to it was a fuzzy photograph of a jellyfish.

Imagine the body free of its anchors,
        the free-swimming,
a locomotion propelling us, pulse by pulse,
but here I am: the slow caboose of clumsy effort.

When the magician's wife died, how could they be sure
he hadn't just turned her into ether, released her
        like a white bird begging for the sky outside the cage?

Creeley says, *The plan is the body*. What if he's wrong?

I am always in too many worlds, sand sifting through my hands,
      another me speeding through the air, another me waving
from a train window watching you
        waving from a train window watching me.

CANNIBAL WOMAN

I'm looking for the right words, but all I can think of is:
       parachute or ice water.

There's nothing but this sailboat inside me, slowly trying to catch
a wind, maybe there's an old man on it, maybe a small child,

all I know is they'd like to go somewhere. They'd like to see the sail

straighten, go tense, and take them someplace. But instead they wait,
a little tender wave comes and leaves them
       right where they were all along.

How did this happen? No wind I can conjure anymore.

My father told me the story of a woman larger than a mountain,
who crushed redwoods with her feet, who could swim a whole lake

in two strokes—she ate human flesh and terrorized the people.

I loved that story. She was bigger than any monster, or Bigfoot,
       or Loch Ness creature—

a woman who was like weather, as enormous as a storm.

He'd tell me how she walked through the woods, each tree
coming down, branch to sawdust, leaf to skeleton, each mountain
       pulverized to dust.

Then they set a trap. A hole so deep she could not climb out of it.

(I have known that trap.)

Then people set her on fire with torches. So she could not eat them
anymore, could not steal their children or ruin their trees.

I liked this part too. The fire. I imagined how it burned her mouth,
her skin, and how she tried to stand but couldn't, how it almost felt

good to her—as if something was finally meeting her desire with desire.

The part I didn't like was the end, how each ash that flew up in the night
        became a mosquito, how she is still all around us
in the dark, multiplied.

I've worried my whole life that my father told me this because
she is my anger: first comes this hunger, then abyss, then fire,

and then a nearly invisible fly made of ash goes on and on eating mouthful
after mouthful of those I love.

WIFE

I'm not yet comfortable with the word,
its short clean woosh that sounds like
life. At dinner last night my single girls
said in admonition, *It's not wife-approved*
about a friend's upcoming trip. Their
eyes rolled up and over and out of their
pretty young heads. Wife, why does it
sound like a job? *I want a wife*, the famous
feminist wrote, *a wife who will keep my
clothes clean, ironed, mended, replaced
when need be.* A word that could be made
easily into maid. A wife that does, fixes,
soothes, honors, obeys. Housewife,
fishwife, bad wife, good wife, what's
the word for someone who stares long
into the morning, unable to even fix tea
some days, the kettle steaming over
loud like a train whistle, she who cries
in the mornings, she who tears a hole
in the earth and cannot stop grieving,
the one who wants to love you, but often
isn't good at even that, the one who
doesn't want to be diminished
by how much she wants to be yours.

FROM THE ASH INSIDE THE BONE

Right when all I want to do is tell you a story,
       the way *wiingaashk* (is that the word,

the name for sweetgrass that Kimmerer gives?)
have settled in to the middle raised bed,

the way I greet them in the morning, sometimes
         run my fingers through them like a child's hair,
         right when I wanted to tell you a good thing,

a stone to hold and rub in the pocket like skin,

right then, the sickness comes again. I want to write

of the body as desirous, reedy, fine on the tongue
         on the thigh, but my blood's got the spins again, twice

today the world went bonkers. Cracked, careened,
and I come up all clown and out of whack. My body

can't be trusted. MRI says my brain's hunky-dory
         so it's just these bouts sometimes, the ground rises

straight up, or I'm trying to walk on water,
     except it's not water it's land and it's moving when

it should be something to count on. A field of something
         green and steady. Sleep is familiar, though the birds
are starting earlier and earlier, and I keep dreaming

that the sky's turning to ash, or that I'm falling
through the clouds—tops of pine trees and oceans below.

What does Lorca say? *Compadre, quiero cambiar*
    mi caballo por su casa. Friend, I want to trade this horse

of illness for your house that praises the throat.

I'll settle for these words you gave me: *sweet smoke*
       and I'll plant them into my chest so I can take this

circling spell and light it on fire.

TIME IS ON FIRE

I meet a physicist at the party and immediately
ask him if it's true that time doesn't exist, time
being important to me. Even now, I'm older,
time's crypt and wish curl around me like ghost wind.
He doesn't answer so maybe I don't exist. One day:
nothing. Another: mushrooms or mildew, or some
inching sprout, or some leaf gone black and dead.
Time does that. The arrow we ride into the now,
then into the future, does not pull out of the skin
backward. Or does it? The past is happening.
Pampas grass slicing the thumb before the dozer
came and cut the grass out like a cancer, my old cat
Smoke leaving dead birds on the garden posts,
the first man, the first woman, the madrone's rust-
colored berries of fall, each second is in me. The arrow
we ride like a horse, mute and fast, retraces and races,
so that right now even as my valley burns, it rewinds
too, each black ash rubble pile pulls itself back
into a dear home, a living cat leaps into the understory,
and in the soft yellow hills the first flame goes out.

AFTER THE FIRE

You ever think you could cry so hard
that there'd be nothing left in you, like
how the wind shakes a tree in a storm
until every part of it is run through with
wind? I live in the low parts now, most
days a little hazy with fever and waiting
for the water to stop shivering out of the
body. Funny thing about grief, its hold
is so bright and determined like a flame,
like something almost worth living for.

LOSING

After your father gets lost for the third time,
        you get angry because he won't answer his phone.

Part of me wants him to stay lost. God, what has stolen my generosity?

He pours a bowl of cereal and milk and leaves the refrigerator door open.
        He calls you boss and me mother. *Yes, Mother,* he says and rolls

his eyes when I tell him to eat something, to clean up after himself.

Would I be more patient with a child? Would I love the smallness
        of a life more than the gone-ness of the mind? Yes.

I don't know what to do with him, so I cook elaborately—
        pea salad with blanched red onions, radishes and asparagus,
scalloped potatoes, all good things that come from the ground.

He eats the mini eggs I've left for guests until they're gone;
        he says, *How do you feel about abortion?*

I explain how you can eat violets, and dandelions, and wild chives,
so that we almost have an edible lawn. He says he hates birds.

I laugh and ask him, *How can you hate birds?*

He says he hates them because they're everywhere, they are all over,
everywhere you look, and we look up at the sky together.

Turns out he's right, those damn things are everywhere.

THE LAST DROP

You've just left your dad in Virginia with your brother after taking him to the neurologist to confirm that it is, in fact, Alzheimer's. Now, you're driving to New York to get your dead ex-girlfriend's cats who need a home and even though we weren't planning on cats, they're fifteen and who's gonna take them and you know them already and why not give some animals a home even if it's another twenty hours of driving there and back? I tell Manuel about your travels and he says, *It's a good premise for a horrible road trip dark comedy movie.* And there is something funny about it all. Your father hates cats, but they love him. And I spent a long time envious of your ex-girlfriend's beauty and now I only miss her and want to love her cats for her. My memoir could be titled *Everything Was Fine until It Wasn't.* My memoir could be called *I Thought I Wanted a Baby but All I Got Was Your Dead Ex-Girlfriend's Two Old Cats.* My memoir could be called *Before the Wedding You Must Suffer a Little.* My mother's motto is "Nothing Is Easy" and I tease her for it, but it's true. Before he left, your dad said he didn't understand the saying "Good to the last drop." *Does that mean the last drop is bad?* he asked. *No,* I reassured. *It means all of it is good, every single drop of it is good.*

We were quick to tell each other what we wanted. I said I want to be cremated and then I want my ashes to be tossed in the Pacific and the Atlantic. He said I was greedy for wanting both coasts, but he'd do it. I made it specific: Herring Cove in Cape Cod and Salmon Creek on the Sonoma coast (but also, I was thinking of the Calabazas Creek in Glen Ellen). He said any horse farm would do for him, and then he corrected himself to just any pretty pasture. He said we don't believe in the afterlife. I stopped him and said, *I don't believe in God, but I do have some very interesting thoughts concerning ghosts.* What he was trying to say, if I'd stop talking about ghosts for once, is that it's important to have a spot to visit: a tree, a rock, any place where you can think of that person. We've got her two old cats downstairs now, hiding behind the water heater, the stairs, hissing and purring both. Last night, I dreamt that she didn't like me, wouldn't let me in a car that everyone else was getting into. Or rather she took the last seat in the car and everyone drove off without me. But this morning, I kissed the man she used to love and one of her cats crawled into my lap.

SPARROW, WHAT DID YOU SAY?

A whole day without speaking,
rain, then sun, then rain again,
a few plants in the ground, newbie
leaves tucked in black soil, and I think
I'm good at this, this being alone
in the world, the watching of things
growing, this older me, the she
in comfortable shoes and no time
for dishes, the she who spent
an hour trying to figure out that the bird
with a three-note descending call
is just a sparrow. What would I
do with a kid here? Teach her
to plant, watch her like I do
the lettuce leaves, tenderly, place
her palms in the earth, part her
black hair like planting a seed? Or
would I selfishly demand this day
back, a full untethered day trying
to figure out what bird was calling
to me and why.

NOTES & ACKNOWLEDGMENTS

My deep appreciation goes out to my friends and mentors who put up with my questions, my moods, and my always asking for advice. I'd particularly like to thank those people who have read almost all of these poems in many different forms and have made them better for their attention and care: my stepfather Brady T. Brady, my mother Stacia Brady, Jennifer L. Knox, Jason Schneiderman, Adam Clay, Michael Robins, Matthew Zapruder, Vaughan Fielder, Rob McQuilkin, Trish Harnetiaux, and Heather Grossmann. Thank you to my teachers who are with me in everything I do. Thank you to Natalie Diaz for the letter-poems we wrote back and forth to each other for a year. Thank you to Diana Lee Craig and Jeff Baker for giving me a home on Moon Mountain to write and to breathe. Thank you to my father, to Linda, and to my brothers who, for some reason, never stop believing in me. Thank you to all the large-hearted people at Milkweed Editions who have been my guides and my pit crew. Thank you to my editor, Wayne Miller, whose keen eye is unsurpassed. Thank you to my mother, whose stunning paintings grace all of my book covers. Finally, thank you to my husband, Lucas, who encourages me to write everything about our lives even when it's the hard stuff. I am forever grateful for this life.

Thank you to the editors of the following journals, in which the poems of this book, sometimes in earlier versions, first appeared.

Academy of American Poets, poets.org: "The Leash," "Instructions on Not Giving Up," "Notes on the Below"

American Poetry Review: "The Year of the Goldfinches," "Almost Forty," "Sundown & All the Damage Done," "It's Harder"

Buzzfeed: "A New National Anthem"

Copper Nickel: "The Contract Says: We'd Like the Conversation to Be Bilingual"

Guernica: "On a Lamppost Long Ago"

Lit Hub: "Prey"

MAKE: "On a Pink Moon," "Trying," "The Raincoat"

Mississippi Review: "Love Poem with Apologies for My Appearance," "The Last Thing"

Monstering: "Wonder Woman"

National/Amtrak: "Of Roots & Roamers"

New Yorker: "The Burying Beetle," "Overpass," "Sway," "From the Ash inside the Bone," "Sometimes I Think My Body Leaves a Shape in the Air," "Cargo"

New York Observer: "How We Are Made"

Poetry in Motion/MTA Subway/InDigest: "A Name"

Prairie Schooner: "American Pharoah"

Southern Indiana Review: "The Millionth Dream of Your Return," "Dream of Destruction"

SWWIM: "Cannibal Woman"

Tin House: "Maybe I'll Be Another Kind of Mother," "Would You Rather," "Carrying"

Tupelo Quarterly: "The Light the Living See," "Sparrow, What Did You Say?"

Typo: "Full Gallop"

Virginia Quarterly Review: "After His Ex Died," "Losing," "The Vulture & the Body," "Sacred Objects"

Washington Square Review: "What I Want to Remember," "What I Didn't Know Before"

Waxwing Literary Journal: "Late Summer After a Panic Attack," "Bust," "The Visitor"

What Rough Beasts: "Killing Methods"

"The Leash" was awarded the Pushcart Prize (2016).

"Killing Methods" is anthologized in *Resistance, Rebellion, Life: 50 Poems Now*. "A New National Anthem" is anthologized in *The Mighty Stream: Poems in Celebration of Martin Luther King*. "The Leash" is anthologized in *Bullets into Bells: Poets & Citizens Respond to Gun Violence*.

"Sway," "From the Ash inside the Bone," "Sometimes I Think My Body Leaves a Shape in the Air," and "Cargo" were all written as letter-poems to Natalie Diaz as part of the anthology *They Said: A Multi-Genre Anthology of Contemporary Collaborative Writing*.

Lucas Marquardt

ADA LIMÓN is the author of four books of poetry, including *Bright Dead Things*, which was named a finalist for the National Book Award, the National Book Critics Circle Award, and the Kingsley Tufts Poetry Award. Her work has appeared in numerous publications including the *New Yorker*, the *New York Times*, *Tin House*, and *American Poetry Review*.

Typeset in Garamond
by Mary Austin Speaker

Adobe Garamond is based upon the typefaces first created by
Parisian printer Claude Garamond in the sixteenth century.
Garamond based his typeface on the handwriting of Angelo
Vergecio, librarian to King Francis I. The font's slenderness makes
it not only highly readable but also one of the most eco-friendly
typefaces available because it requires less ink than similar faces.
Robert Slimbach created this digital version of Garamond for
Adobe in 1989 and his font has become one of the most
widely used typefaces in print.